How to Paint - Prepare, Choose Colors, Apply Techniques, and Use Tools

Surface Prep Techniques, Color Selection Tips, Paint Application Methods, and Essential Painting Tools for Flawless Results

Jack Homer

Copyright © 2024 by Jack Homer

All rights reserved. No part of this publication may be reproduced, distributed, or transmitted in any form or by any means, including photocopying, recording, or other electronic or mechanical methods, without the prior written permission of the author, except in the case of brief quotations embodied in critical reviews and certain other noncommercial uses permitted by copyright law.

Table of Contents

Introduction

Chapter 1: Surface Preparation
  - Cleaning and Repairing Surfaces
  - Sanding and Smoothing Techniques
  - Priming for Optimal Results

Chapter 2: Color Selection Tips
  - Exploring Color Psychology
  - Choosing the Right Color Scheme for Your Space
  - Testing and Finalizing Color Choices

Chapter 3: Paint Application Methods
  - Brushing Techniques
  - Rolling Techniques
  - Spraying Methods for Efficiency

Chapter 4: Essential Painting Tools
  - Brushes, Rollers, and Applicators
  - Masking and Protective Equipment
  - Specialty Tools for Specific Surfaces

Chapter 5: Troubleshooting Common Issues
  - Dealing with Drips and Runs
  - Achieving Smooth Finishes
  - Addressing Uneven Coverage

Chapter 6: Advanced Techniques and Finishing Touches
  - Faux Finishes and Decorative Painting
  - Adding Texture to Walls
  - Finalizing Details for Professional Results

Conclusion

Introduction

Before you can create a masterpiece on your walls, you need to lay the groundwork for success. Surface preparation is the crucial first step in achieving a flawless finish that will stand the test of time. In this chapter, we'll walk you through the essential tasks of cleaning and repairing surfaces, ensuring that your canvas is smooth, pristine, and ready for painting.

1. Cleaning Surfaces:
- Start by removing any furniture or decorations from the area you'll be painting. This will give you ample space to work and prevent accidental damage to your belongings.
- Dust and cobwebs can wreak havoc on your paint job, so grab a duster or vacuum with a brush attachment and thoroughly clean the walls and ceilings. Pay special attention to corners and crevices where dust tends to accumulate.
- For stubborn dirt or grease stains, mix a solution of warm water and mild detergent. Use a sponge or cloth to gently scrub the affected areas, then rinse with clean water and allow to dry completely.
- Don't forget about mold and mildew—these unsightly intruders can not only ruin your paint job but also pose health risks. Treat any mold or mildew with a solution of one part bleach to three parts water, then scrub and rinse as necessary.
- Once the surfaces are clean and dry, inspect them for any cracks, holes, or other imperfections that need to be addressed before painting.

2. *Repairing Surfaces:*

- Patching holes and cracks is essential for achieving a smooth, seamless finish. Use a lightweight spackling compound or joint compound to fill in any small holes or cracks, smoothing it out with a putty knife.
- For larger holes or damaged areas, you may need to use a patching compound or drywall repair kit. Follow the manufacturer's instructions carefully, and allow ample time for the patch to dry before sanding.
- Sanding is the final step in surface preparation, and it's crucial for ensuring a uniform surface for painting. Use a fine-grit sandpaper or sanding block to smooth out any rough patches or uneven surfaces, working in a circular motion until the entire area is smooth to the touch.
- After sanding, be sure to wipe down the surfaces with a damp cloth to remove any dust or debris. This will ensure that your paint adheres properly and results in a flawless finish.

By following these simple steps for cleaning and repairing surfaces, you'll set yourself up for painting success. With a smooth, pristine canvas to work with, you can unleash your creativity and bring your vision to life on the walls of your home. So roll up your sleeves and get ready to transform your space—your freshly painted oasis awaits!

Chapter 1
Surface Preparation
Cleaning and Repairing Surfaces

Sanding and smoothing techniques are vital steps in the surface preparation process that can significantly impact the quality of your paint job. Whether you're dealing with rough patches, uneven surfaces, or old paint residue, proper sanding techniques can help achieve a smooth and flawless canvas for painting. In this section, we'll delve into the intricacies of sanding and smoothing, equipping you with the knowledge and skills to tackle any surface with confidence.

1. Assess the Surface:
Before diving into sanding, take a moment to assess the condition of the surface you'll be working on. Identify any rough patches, bumps, or imperfections that need attention. Additionally, if you're working with previously painted surfaces, check for flaking or peeling paint that may require removal before sanding.

2. Choose the Right Sandpaper:
Selecting the appropriate sandpaper grit is crucial for achieving the desired results. Coarse-grit sandpaper (around 80 to 120 grit) is ideal for removing rough patches, old paint, or imperfections. As you progress, gradually switch to finer-grit sandpaper (150 to 220 grit) for smoothing and refining the surface. Keep in mind that using too coarse a grit initially can leave deep scratches, while starting with too fine a grit may not effectively remove imperfections.

3. Sanding Techniques:
- Begin by securing the sandpaper to a sanding block or a sanding tool for better control and even pressure distribution.
- Use long, smooth strokes in the direction of the grain (if applicable) to avoid creating scratches or gouges in the surface.
- Apply gentle but consistent pressure, letting the sandpaper do the work. Avoid pressing too hard, as this can result in uneven sanding and damage to the surface.
- For curved or contoured surfaces, consider using flexible sanding tools or sanding sponges to ensure thorough and even sanding.

4. Addressing Imperfections:
- Pay close attention to areas with visible imperfections, such as dents, scratches, or uneven patches. Use a finer-grit sandpaper to smooth out these areas gradually, blending them seamlessly with the surrounding surface.
- If you encounter stubborn imperfections that resist sanding, consider using a filler or putty to fill in the gaps before sanding again. Allow the filler to dry completely before sanding and smoothing.

5. Dust Removal:
- After sanding, thoroughly clean the surface to remove any dust or debris using a damp cloth or vacuum with a brush attachment. This step is crucial for ensuring proper paint adhesion and a smooth finish.
- Additionally, consider using a tack cloth to remove any remaining dust particles that may be invisible to the naked eye. This will ensure a pristine surface for painting.

By mastering the art of sanding and smoothing techniques, you'll be well-equipped to tackle any surface preparation challenge with ease. With a smooth and flawless canvas to work with, you can unleash your creativity and achieve professional-quality results with every paint job. So grab your sandpaper and sanding tools—it's time to elevate your painting game and transform your space into a masterpiece!

Sanding and Smoothing Techniques

Sanding and smoothing techniques are vital steps in the surface preparation process that can significantly impact the quality of your paint job. Whether you're dealing with rough patches, uneven surfaces, or old paint residue, proper sanding techniques can help achieve a smooth and flawless canvas for painting. In this section, we'll delve into the intricacies of sanding and smoothing, equipping you with the knowledge and skills to tackle any surface with confidence.

1. Assess the Surface:
Before diving into sanding, take a moment to assess the condition of the surface you'll be working on. Identify any rough patches, bumps, or imperfections that need attention. Additionally, if you're working with previously painted surfaces, check for flaking or peeling paint that may require removal before sanding.

2. Choose the Right Sandpaper:
Selecting the appropriate sandpaper grit is crucial for achieving the desired results. Coarse-grit sandpaper (around 80 to 120 grit) is ideal for removing rough patches, old paint, or imperfections. As you progress, gradually switch to finer-grit sandpaper (150 to 220 grit) for smoothing and refining the surface. Keep in mind that using too coarse a grit initially can leave deep scratches, while starting with too fine a grit may not effectively remove imperfections.

3. Sanding Techniques:
- Begin by securing the sandpaper to a sanding block or a sanding tool for better control and even pressure distribution.

- Use long, smooth strokes in the direction of the grain (if applicable) to avoid creating scratches or gouges in the surface.
- Apply gentle but consistent pressure, letting the sandpaper do the work. Avoid pressing too hard, as this can result in uneven sanding and damage to the surface.
- For curved or contoured surfaces, consider using flexible sanding tools or sanding sponges to ensure thorough and even sanding.

4. Addressing Imperfections:
- Pay close attention to areas with visible imperfections, such as dents, scratches, or uneven patches. Use a finer-grit sandpaper to smooth out these areas gradually, blending them seamlessly with the surrounding surface.
- If you encounter stubborn imperfections that resist sanding, consider using a filler or putty to fill in the gaps before sanding again. Allow the filler to dry completely before sanding and smoothing.

5. Dust Removal:
- After sanding, thoroughly clean the surface to remove any dust or debris using a damp cloth or vacuum with a brush attachment. This step is crucial for ensuring proper paint adhesion and a smooth finish.
- Additionally, consider using a tack cloth to remove any remaining dust particles that may be invisible to the naked eye. This will ensure a pristine surface for painting.

By mastering the art of sanding and smoothing techniques, you'll be well-equipped to tackle any surface preparation challenge with ease. With a smooth and flawless canvas to work with, you can unleash your creativity and achieve professional-quality results with every paint job. So grab your sandpaper and sanding tools—it's time to elevate your painting game and transform your space into a masterpiece!

Priming for Optimal Results

Priming is a critical step in the painting process that sets the stage for optimal adhesion, durability, and finish quality. While it may seem like an optional step, especially for surfaces that seem smooth or have been previously painted, priming ensures that your paint job stands the test of time. In this section, we'll delve into the importance of priming and provide a detailed explanation of the priming process for achieving flawless results.

1. Understanding the Purpose of Priming:
Priming serves multiple purposes, all of which contribute to achieving optimal results with your paint job:
- Promotes Adhesion: Primers create a bonding surface that helps paint adhere more effectively to the substrate, reducing the risk of peeling, flaking, or chipping over time.
- Seals and Protects: Primers seal porous surfaces, such as bare wood or drywall, preventing them from absorbing excessive amounts of paint and resulting in uneven coverage. Additionally, primers can block stains, tannins, and other surface contaminants, ensuring a smooth and uniform finish.
- Enhances Paint Performance: By providing a uniform base layer, primers improve the appearance and durability of the final paint finish, allowing for better color saturation, sheen uniformity, and resistance to moisture, mildew, and other environmental factors.

2. Selecting the Right Primer:

Choosing the appropriate primer for your project is crucial for achieving optimal results. Consider the following factors when selecting a primer:

- Surface Type: Different surfaces require specific types of primers tailored to their unique characteristics. For example, bare wood typically requires a wood primer, while metal surfaces may benefit from a rust-inhibiting primer.
- Paint Compatibility: Ensure that the primer is compatible with the type of paint you'll be using, whether it's latex, oil-based, or specialty paint.
- Special Considerations: If you're dealing with stains, odors, or other surface issues, opt for a specialty primer designed to address these specific concerns.

3. Application Techniques:

Once you've selected the appropriate primer, follow these steps for proper application:

- Prepare the Surface: Clean the surface thoroughly to remove any dust, dirt, grease, or other contaminants that may interfere with adhesion. Sand glossy surfaces lightly to improve primer adhesion.
- Stir the Primer: Before application, stir the primer thoroughly to ensure uniform consistency and distribution of pigments and additives.
- Apply the Primer: Use a high-quality brush, roller, or sprayer to apply the primer evenly to the surface. Work in manageable sections, maintaining a wet edge to prevent lap marks and ensure uniform coverage.

- Allow Drying Time: Follow the manufacturer's instructions for drying times between coats and before applying paint. Typically, primers require at least 24 hours to cure fully before painting.

4. Sanding and Additional Coats:
After the primer has dried, lightly sand the surface with fine-grit sandpaper to smooth out any imperfections and ensure optimal paint adhesion. Depending on the condition of the surface and the type of primer used, you may need to apply additional coats of primer for maximum coverage and performance.

5. Cleanup and Safety:
After completing the priming process, clean your brushes, rollers, and other tools with soap and water or paint thinner, depending on the type of primer used. Dispose of any leftover primer and solvent materials according to local regulations and safety guidelines.

By prioritizing priming as an essential step in your painting process, you'll ensure that your paint job not only looks great but also lasts longer and withstands the rigors of daily life. With a properly primed surface, you can unleash your creativity and achieve flawless results with every brushstroke. So don't skip the primer—invest in the foundation of your paint job and enjoy the lasting benefits of a professional-quality finish.

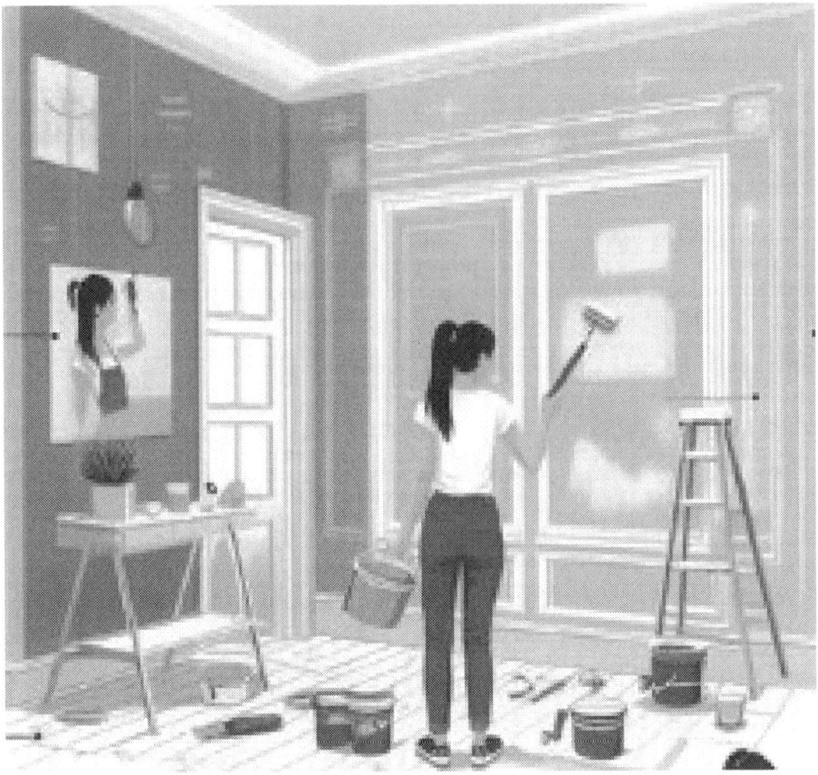

Chapter 2
Color Selection Tips
Exploring Color Psychology

Color psychology plays a significant role in influencing our emotions, perceptions, and behaviors. When it comes to painting interiors, understanding the psychological effects of color can help you create spaces that evoke specific moods, enhance functionality, and reflect your personal style. In this section, we'll explore the fascinating world of color psychology and provide detailed insights into how different colors can impact your home environment.

1. Understanding Color Psychology:
Color psychology is the study of how different colors affect human emotions, attitudes, and behaviors. Each color has unique psychological associations that can evoke specific feelings and perceptions:
- Warm Colors: Warm colors such as red, orange, and yellow are often associated with energy, warmth, and passion. These colors can create a sense of excitement and stimulation, making them ideal for spaces where you want to promote creativity, activity, and social interaction.
- Cool Colors: Cool colors like blue, green, and purple are known for their calming and soothing effects. These colors evoke feelings of relaxation, tranquility, and serenity, making them well-suited for bedrooms, bathrooms, and other areas where you want to promote a sense of peace and harmony.

- Neutral Colors: Neutral colors such as white, beige, and gray provide a versatile backdrop that can complement any design style. These colors are often associated with simplicity, elegance, and sophistication, making them ideal for creating a timeless and cohesive aesthetic in your home.

2. *Applying Color Psychology in Interior Design:*
When selecting colors for your interior spaces, consider the following principles of color psychology to achieve the desired atmosphere and mood:
- Functionality: Think about the function of each room and how you want people to feel when they enter it. For example, vibrant and energizing colors may be suitable for a home office or gym, while soft and soothing hues may be more appropriate for a bedroom or living room.
- Personal Preference: Consider your own preferences and how you want to feel in each space. Choose colors that resonate with you personally and reflect your unique personality and style.
- Balance and Contrast: Experiment with different color combinations to create visual interest and harmony in your home. Balance bold and vibrant colors with softer neutrals or use contrasting colors to highlight architectural features and create focal points.
- Lighting and Environment: Take into account the natural lighting conditions and existing elements in your home, such as furniture, flooring, and decor. Certain colors may appear different under various lighting conditions, so test paint samples in different areas of the room to see how they look throughout the day.

3. Practical Tips for Choosing Colors:
To simplify the process of selecting colors for your home, consider the following practical tips:
- Start Small: Begin by choosing a few key colors that you love and build your color palette around them. Consider incorporating different shades and tones of the same color to create depth and dimension.
- Test Paint Samples: Before committing to a color scheme, test paint samples on your walls to see how they look in different lighting conditions and alongside other elements in the room.
- Seek Inspiration: Look for inspiration in magazines, websites, and social media platforms to discover new color trends, palettes, and design ideas. Create mood boards or color swatches to help visualize your vision and make informed decisions.
- Trust Your Instincts: Ultimately, trust your instincts and choose colors that resonate with you emotionally and reflect the mood and ambiance you want to create in your home.

By incorporating the principles of color psychology into your interior design process, you can create spaces that not only look beautiful but also feel harmonious, welcoming, and inspiring. Whether you prefer bold and vibrant hues or soft and subtle tones, understanding the psychological effects of color empowers you to create environments that truly enhance your well-being and enrich your daily life. So embrace the power of color and let your imagination run wild as you transform your home into a reflection of your unique personality and style.

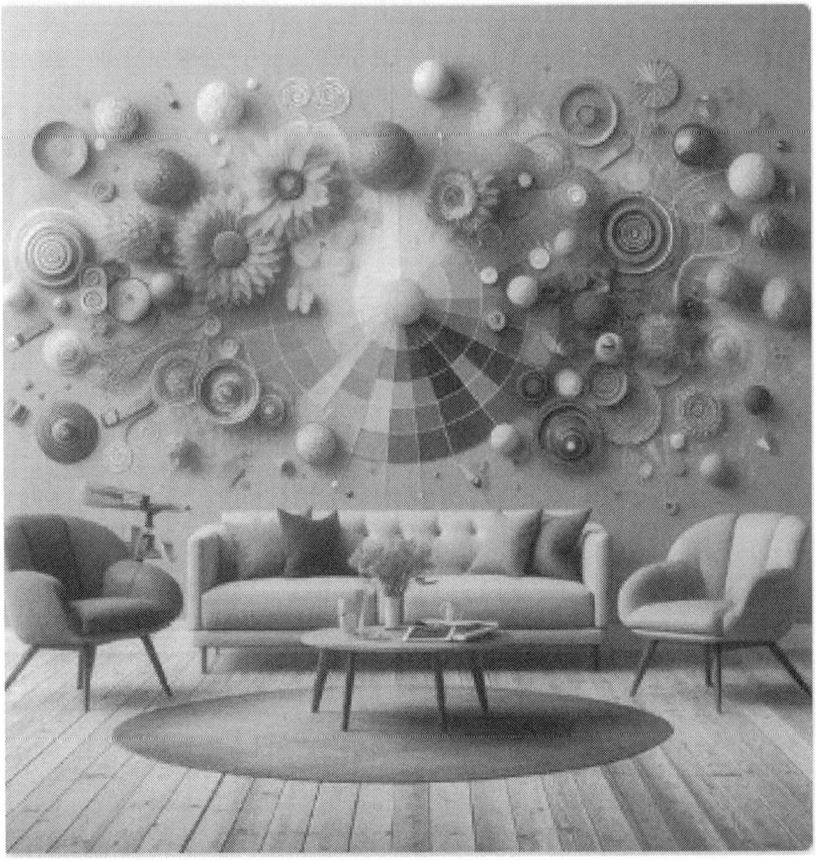

Choosing the Right Color Scheme for Your Space

Choosing the right color scheme for your space is a crucial step in interior design that sets the tone for the entire room. The colors you select can influence the mood, ambiance, and functionality of the space, so it's essential to consider factors such as personal preference, room function, and desired atmosphere. In this section, we'll provide a detailed explanation of how to choose the perfect color scheme for your space, guiding you through the process step by step.

1. Consider the Room's Function:
Before selecting a color scheme, consider how the room will be used and the atmosphere you want to create:
- For high-traffic areas such as living rooms and kitchens, consider using warm, inviting colors like shades of beige, taupe, or soft gray to promote comfort and relaxation while encouraging social interaction.
- In spaces dedicated to rest and relaxation, such as bedrooms or reading nooks, opt for cool, calming colors like shades of blue, green, or lavender to create a serene and peaceful environment conducive to unwinding and rejuvenation.
- Home offices and creative spaces benefit from energizing colors like shades of yellow, orange, or red, which can promote productivity, creativity, and focus.

2. Understand Color Theory:
Familiarize yourself with basic color theory principles to create harmonious and visually appealing color schemes:

- Monochromatic: Choose varying shades and tones of the same color for a cohesive and sophisticated look. This approach creates depth and visual interest without overwhelming the space.
- Analogous: Select colors that are adjacent to each other on the color wheel, such as blue and green or yellow and orange. This creates a harmonious and cohesive color scheme with subtle variations.
- Complementary: Pair colors that are opposite each other on the color wheel, such as blue and orange or purple and yellow. This creates a bold and dynamic color scheme with striking contrast.
- Triadic: Choose three colors evenly spaced around the color wheel, such as red, yellow, and blue. This approach creates a vibrant and balanced color scheme with a diverse range of hues.

3. Consider Existing Elements:

Take into account existing elements in the room, such as furniture, flooring, and architectural features, when selecting a color scheme:

- If you have a statement piece of furniture or artwork, consider using its colors as inspiration for your color scheme. Pull out key colors and use them as accents throughout the room to create a cohesive and unified look.
- If you have neutral or monochromatic furnishings, consider using bold or vibrant colors on the walls or accessories to add personality and visual interest to the space.

4. Test Paint Samples:
Before committing to a color scheme, test paint samples on the walls to see how they look in different lighting conditions and alongside existing furnishings:
- Paint small sections of the walls with your chosen colors and observe how they appear throughout the day as natural light changes. Consider how the colors interact with each other and whether they evoke the desired mood and ambiance.
- Take into account how the colors complement or contrast with existing elements in the room and adjust your color scheme accordingly.

5. Trust Your Instincts:
Ultimately, trust your instincts and choose colors that resonate with you emotionally and reflect your personal style and taste:
- Don't be afraid to experiment with different color combinations and shades until you find the perfect balance. Remember that color is subjective, and what works for one person may not work for another.
- Listen to your intuition and select colors that make you feel happy, comfortable, and inspired. Your home should be a reflection of your personality and lifestyle, so choose colors that speak to you on a personal level.

By following these steps and guidelines for choosing the right color scheme for your space, you can create rooms that not only look beautiful but also feel harmonious, welcoming, and inviting. Whether you prefer bold and vibrant hues or soft and subtle tones, understanding the principles of color selection empowers you to transform your home into a reflection of your unique personality and style. So embrace the power of color and let your creativity shine as you design spaces that inspire and delight.

Testing and Finalizing Color Choices

Testing and finalizing color choices is a crucial step in the interior design process, ensuring that the colors you select for your space harmonize with each other and create the desired atmosphere. By testing paint samples and evaluating them in the context of your room's lighting and existing elements, you can confidently make informed decisions and achieve a cohesive and visually appealing color scheme. In this section, we'll provide a detailed explanation of how to effectively test and finalize color choices for your space, guiding you through the process step by step.

1. Gather Inspiration:
Before testing paint samples, gather inspiration from various sources such as interior design magazines, websites, social media platforms, and home decor stores. Create a mood board or color palette that reflects the aesthetic and atmosphere you want to achieve in your space. Consider factors such as personal style, room function, and existing decor when selecting colors.

2. Select Paint Samples:
Once you have a clear vision of your desired color palette, select paint samples in the colors you're considering for your space. Many paint stores offer small sample pots or paint chips that you can take home to test on your walls. Choose a variety of shades and tones within your chosen color scheme to see how they look in different lighting conditions and alongside existing furnishings.

3. Test Paint Samples:
Before applying paint samples to your walls, prepare the surface by cleaning and priming it if necessary. Paint small sections of the walls with each sample color, using a brush or roller to apply an even coat. Allow the paint to dry completely before evaluating the colors.

4. Evaluate in Different Lighting Conditions:
Observe how the paint samples look in various lighting conditions throughout the day, including natural daylight and artificial lighting. Colors can appear different under different lighting sources and intensities, so it's essential to consider how they will look in your specific environment. Pay attention to how the colors change in the morning, afternoon, and evening, as well as how they interact with existing elements in the room.

5. Consider Existing Elements:
Take into account existing elements in the room, such as furniture, flooring, and architectural features, when evaluating paint samples. Consider how the colors complement or contrast with these elements and whether they enhance the overall aesthetic of the space. Look for colors that create a cohesive and harmonious look, tying together the various elements in the room.

6. Finalize Color Choices:
Based on your evaluations and observations, narrow down your choices to a select few colors that best meet your criteria and preferences. Consider factors such as mood, ambiance, functionality, and personal style when making your final decision.

Trust your instincts and select colors that resonate with you emotionally and reflect the vision you have for your space.

7. Purchase Paint and Accessories:
Once you've finalized your color choices, purchase the necessary paint and painting accessories to complete your project. Consider factors such as paint finish, quantity needed, and any additional supplies required for painting, such as brushes, rollers, and drop cloths. Be sure to consult with a paint specialist or interior designer if you have any questions or concerns about your selections.

8. Test Again (Optional):
If you're still uncertain about your color choices or want to confirm your decisions before committing to a full paint job, consider testing the selected colors again in a larger area of the room. Paint larger swatches or sections of the walls with your chosen colors and evaluate them over a few days to ensure they meet your expectations and preferences.

By following these steps and guidelines for testing and finalizing color choices, you can confidently select colors that enhance the beauty and functionality of your space while reflecting your personal style and taste. Whether you prefer bold and vibrant hues or soft and subtle tones, taking the time to test and evaluate paint samples ensures that you achieve the perfect color scheme for your home. So trust your instincts, experiment with different options, and enjoy the process of transforming your space with color.

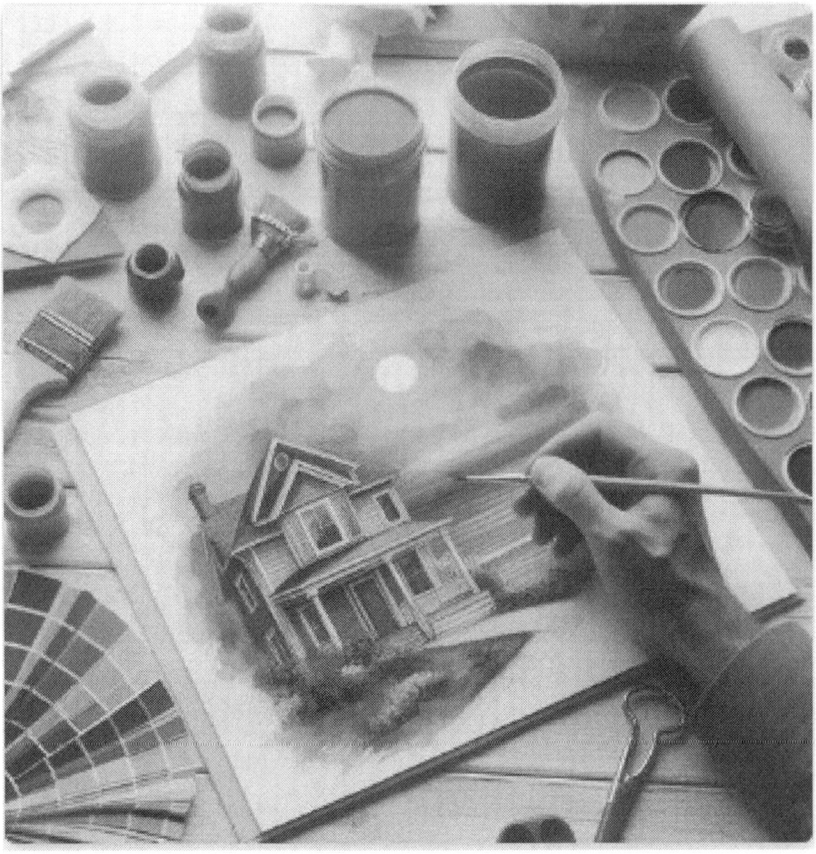

Chapter 3
Paint Application Methods

Brushing Techniques

Painting with brushes is one of the most traditional and versatile methods for applying paint to surfaces. Whether you're painting walls, trim, or furniture, mastering brushing techniques is essential for achieving smooth, even coverage and professional-quality results. In this section, we'll provide an in-depth explanation of brushing techniques, guiding you through the process step by step to ensure a flawless finish.

1. Choose the Right Brush:
Selecting the appropriate brush for your project is crucial for achieving optimal results. Consider factors such as the type of paint you're using, the surface you're painting, and your personal preference. For most interior painting projects, synthetic bristle brushes are ideal for latex paints, while natural bristle brushes are better suited for oil-based paints. Choose a brush with the appropriate size and shape for the area you'll be painting, such as a flat brush for large surfaces or an angled brush for trim and detail work.

2. Prepare the Paint:
Before you begin painting, ensure that your paint is properly mixed and thinned to the desired consistency. Pour a small amount of paint into a paint tray or bucket, and use a stir stick to mix it thoroughly. If necessary, add a small amount of water or paint thinner to achieve the desired consistency for smooth application.

3. Load the Brush:

Dip the bristles of the brush into the paint, and gently tap off any excess on the side of the paint tray. Avoid overloading the brush with paint, as this can lead to drips, runs, and uneven coverage. Instead, aim for a moderate amount of paint on the brush, ensuring that the bristles are evenly coated for consistent application.

4. Cutting In:

Before painting the main areas of the wall or surface, use a technique called cutting in to paint the edges and corners with precision. Dip the tip of the brush into the paint, and carefully draw a straight line along the edge of the surface, using steady and controlled movements. Work in small sections, overlapping each stroke slightly to ensure even coverage and a seamless transition between painted and unpainted areas.

5. Painting the Surface:

Once you've cut in around the edges, use broad, sweeping strokes to paint the main areas of the surface. Hold the brush at a slight angle to the surface, and apply the paint with smooth, even pressure. Work from top to bottom and from one side to the other, overlapping each stroke slightly to avoid visible lines or streaks. Keep a wet edge as you work to ensure seamless blending between sections and minimize the risk of lap marks.

6. Feathering and Blending:
To achieve a smooth and seamless finish, use a technique called feathering to blend the paint strokes together. Lightly drag the brush over the painted surface in a long, sweeping motion, feathering out the edges of each stroke to eliminate any visible lines or brush marks. Work quickly and continuously to maintain a wet edge and prevent the paint from drying before you can blend it.

7. Touching Up:
After the first coat of paint has dried, inspect the surface for any missed spots, drips, or imperfections. Use a small brush to touch up these areas with additional paint, blending them seamlessly with the surrounding surface. Allow the touch-up paint to dry completely before applying additional coats or finishing touches.

8. Cleaning and Maintenance:
After completing your painting project, clean your brushes thoroughly with soap and water or paint thinner, depending on the type of paint you used. Remove any excess paint from the bristles, and reshape them with your fingers or a brush comb. Hang the brushes upside down to dry or store them in a brush keeper to maintain their shape and prolong their lifespan.

By mastering brushing techniques and following these step-by-step instructions, you can achieve professional-quality results with your painting projects. Whether you're painting walls, trim, or furniture, the right brush and proper technique are essential for achieving smooth, even coverage and a flawless finish. So grab your paintbrushes and unleash your creativity—your freshly painted space awaits!

Rolling Techniques

Rolling techniques are essential for achieving smooth, even coverage when painting large surfaces such as walls and ceilings. Whether you're using a roller to apply primer, paint, or a textured finish, mastering rolling techniques is key to achieving professional-quality results. In this section, we'll provide a detailed explanation of rolling techniques, guiding you through the process step by step to ensure a flawless finish.

1. Choose the Right Roller:
Selecting the appropriate roller for your project is crucial for achieving optimal results. Consider factors such as the type of surface you're painting, the texture of the roller cover, and the nap length. For most interior painting projects, a high-quality synthetic roller cover with a medium nap length (3/8 to 1/2 inch) is ideal for smooth and semi-smooth surfaces. Thicker nap lengths are suitable for rough surfaces, while thinner nap lengths are better for smooth surfaces.

2. Prepare the Roller:
Before you begin painting, prepare the roller by attaching it to a roller frame and handle. Slide the roller cover onto the frame and secure it in place with the end caps or clips. If necessary, use a roller tray liner or disposable tray to hold the paint and minimize cleanup. Roll the roller cover over a piece of masking tape or a lint roller to remove any loose fibers or debris that may affect the finish.

3. *Load the Roller:*
Pour a small amount of paint into the roller tray, filling it no more than halfway to avoid spills and waste. Dip the roller cover into the paint, and roll it back and forth on the textured portion of the tray to evenly distribute the paint and remove any excess. Avoid overloading the roller with paint, as this can lead to drips, runs, and uneven coverage.

4. *Rolling Techniques:*
Once the roller is loaded with paint, use the following techniques to apply the paint to the surface:
- Start by painting a narrow section along the top edge of the wall or ceiling, known as the cut-in line, using a brush or angled paint edger.
- Next, use the roller to paint the main area of the surface, working in small sections from top to bottom and from one side to the other. Use long, smooth strokes to apply the paint evenly, overlapping each stroke slightly to ensure full coverage.
- Apply gentle but consistent pressure as you roll the paint onto the surface, allowing the roller cover to do the work. Avoid pressing too hard, as this can result in uneven application and streaks.
- Roll the roller cover in a W-shaped pattern or zigzag motion to evenly distribute the paint and avoid creating visible lines or streaks. Roll back over the painted section in the opposite direction to smooth out any ridges or texture left by the roller.

5. *Feathering and Blending:*
To achieve a seamless finish, use a technique called feathering to blend the paint strokes together. Lightly roll the roller over the painted surface in a long, sweeping motion, feathering out the edges of each stroke to eliminate any visible lines or roller marks. Work quickly and continuously to maintain a wet edge and prevent the paint from drying before you can blend it.

6. *Touching Up:*
After the first coat of paint has dried, inspect the surface for any missed spots, drips, or imperfections. Use a brush or roller to touch up these areas with additional paint, blending them seamlessly with the surrounding surface. Allow the touch-up paint to dry completely before applying additional coats or finishing touches.

7. *Cleanup and Maintenance:*
After completing your painting project, clean your roller cover thoroughly with soap and water or a roller cleaner, depending on the type of paint you used. Remove any excess paint from the roller cover, and reshape it with your hands or a roller comb. Hang the roller cover upside down to dry or store it in a plastic bag to keep it from drying out.

By mastering rolling techniques and following these step-by-step instructions, you can achieve professional-quality results with your painting projects. Whether you're painting walls, ceilings, or other large surfaces, the right roller and proper technique are essential for achieving smooth, even coverage and a flawless finish. So grab your roller and paint with confidence—your freshly painted space awaits!

Spraying Methods for Efficiency

Spraying methods offer efficient and effective ways to apply paint to large surfaces quickly and evenly. Whether you're painting walls, ceilings, or furniture, mastering spraying techniques can help you achieve professional-quality results with less effort and in less time. In this section, we'll provide a detailed explanation of spraying methods, guiding you through the process step by step to ensure optimal efficiency and a flawless finish.

1. Choose the Right Sprayer:
Selecting the appropriate sprayer for your project is crucial for achieving optimal results. Consider factors such as the type of paint you're using, the size of the surface you're painting, and your budget. There are three main types of paint sprayers:

- Airless Sprayers: Ideal for large surface areas and thick coatings, airless sprayers use high pressure to atomize paint without the need for compressed air. They are suitable for both interior and exterior painting projects and can handle a variety of paint types and viscosities.
- HVLP (High Volume, Low Pressure) Sprayers: HVLP sprayers use low pressure to atomize paint, resulting in less overspray and finer atomization. They are ideal for precision painting and detail work, making them suitable for furniture, trim, and other small-scale projects.
- Compressed Air Sprayers: Compressed air sprayers use compressed air to atomize paint, providing consistent coverage and a smooth finish. They are versatile and can handle a wide range of paint types and viscosities, making them suitable for a variety of projects.

2. Prepare the Sprayer:

Before you begin painting, prepare the sprayer by assembling and adjusting it according to the manufacturer's instructions. Ensure that all components are clean and free of debris, and check for any leaks or malfunctions. Fill the paint reservoir with the appropriate amount of paint, and adjust the spray settings to achieve the desired spray pattern and flow rate.

3. Mask and Protect Surrounding Areas:

Before spraying, mask and protect surrounding areas to prevent overspray and paint splatter. Use painter's tape and plastic sheeting to cover floors, furniture, trim, and any other surfaces you want to protect from paint. Consider using drop cloths or tarps to cover larger areas and minimize cleanup.

4. Test and Adjust Settings:

Before spraying the main surface, perform a test spray on a scrap piece of cardboard or a small inconspicuous area to ensure that the sprayer is functioning properly and that the paint is atomizing correctly. Adjust the spray settings as needed to achieve the desired spray pattern, coverage, and flow rate. Experiment with different nozzle sizes, spray angles, and pressure settings to find the optimal combination for your project.

5. Spray Technique:

Once you've tested and adjusted the settings, use the following techniques to spray paint efficiently and evenly:
- Hold the sprayer perpendicular to the surface and maintain a consistent distance of 6 to 12 inches for optimal coverage. Avoid holding the sprayer too close, as this can result in drips, runs, and uneven coverage.

- Use smooth, overlapping strokes to apply the paint evenly, working from one side to the other and from top to bottom. Keep the sprayer moving at a steady pace to avoid oversaturation and buildup of paint in one area.
- Adjust the spray pattern and flow rate as needed to accommodate different surface textures and angles. Use a wider spray pattern for larger areas and a narrower pattern for detailed or hard-to-reach areas.
- Pay attention to the direction of the spray and overlap each pass by 50% to ensure full coverage and a seamless finish. Feather out the edges of each pass to blend them together and eliminate any visible lines or streaks.

6. Cleanup and Maintenance:

After completing your painting project, clean the sprayer thoroughly according to the manufacturer's instructions to prevent clogs and malfunctions. Flush out the paint reservoir, nozzle, and other components with water or solvent, depending on the type of paint used. Disassemble the sprayer and clean each component individually, taking care to remove any paint residue or debris. Store the sprayer in a clean, dry place until the next use.

By mastering spraying methods and following these step-by-step instructions, you can achieve professional-quality results with your painting projects while saving time and effort. Whether you're painting walls, ceilings, or furniture, the right sprayer and proper technique are essential for achieving smooth, even coverage and a flawless finish. So grab your sprayer and paint with confidence—your freshly painted space awaits!

Chapter 4
Essential Painting Tools
Brushes, Rollers, and Applicators

Essential painting tools such as brushes, rollers, and applicators are the backbone of any painting project, enabling you to achieve smooth, even coverage and professional-quality results. Whether you're painting walls, trim, or furniture, selecting the right tools and mastering their use is crucial for achieving optimal efficiency and a flawless finish. In this section, we'll provide a detailed explanation of brushes, rollers, and applicators, guiding you through their features, uses, and techniques to ensure success in your painting endeavors.

1. Brushes:
Paint brushes come in a variety of sizes, shapes, and bristle types, each suited for different painting tasks and surfaces. Here's an overview of the most common types of brushes and their uses:

Bristle Types:
- Natural Bristle Brushes: Made from animal hair, such as hog or ox hair, natural bristle brushes are best suited for oil-based paints and varnishes. They provide excellent paint pickup and release and are ideal for painting trim, furniture, and other detailed surfaces.
- Synthetic Bristle Brushes: Made from nylon or polyester filaments, synthetic bristle brushes are suitable for both latex and oil-based paints.

- They offer smooth application, minimal shedding, and easy cleanup, making them versatile and durable for a variety of painting projects.

Brush Shapes:
- Flat Brushes: Flat brushes have a square or rectangular shape with straight edges, making them ideal for painting large, flat surfaces such as walls and ceilings. They provide even coverage and smooth finishes and are available in various sizes to accommodate different surface areas.
- Angled Brushes: Angled brushes have a tapered edge, allowing for precise cutting-in and detail work around corners, edges, and trim. They are commonly used for painting trim, molding, and other intricate areas where accuracy is essential.
- Round Brushes: Round brushes have a circular shape with a pointed tip, making them ideal for painting curves, circles, and detailed shapes. They are versatile and can be used for both large-scale painting and fine detail work.

Techniques:
- Hold the brush firmly but comfortably, gripping it near the ferrule for optimal control and maneuverability.
- Load the brush with paint by dipping the bristles into the paint and tapping off any excess on the side of the paint can or tray.
- Apply the paint using smooth, even strokes, working from top to bottom and from one side to the other. Use long, sweeping motions for large surfaces and smaller, controlled movements for detail work.

- Feather out the edges of each stroke to blend them together and eliminate any visible lines or brush marks.

2. Rollers:

Paint rollers are essential for painting large surface areas quickly and efficiently, providing smooth, uniform coverage with minimal effort. Here's an overview of rollers and their uses:

Roller Covers:
- Nap Length: Roller covers come in various nap lengths, ranging from short (1/4 inch) to long (1 inch or more). Thicker nap lengths are suitable for rough surfaces, while thinner nap lengths are better for smooth surfaces.
- Material: Roller covers are typically made from synthetic materials such as polyester or microfiber, which provide excellent paint pickup and release and are resistant to shedding and matting.

Roller Frames:
- Size: Roller frames come in various sizes to accommodate different roller covers and surface areas. Choose a frame size that matches the width of the roller cover for optimal coverage and efficiency.
- Handle: Roller frames feature a handle for easy maneuverability and control during painting. Look for ergonomic handles with comfortable grips to reduce hand fatigue during extended use.

Techniques:
- Attach the roller cover to the frame by sliding it onto the end and securing it in place with the end caps or clips.
- Load the roller with paint by dipping it into the paint tray and rolling it back and forth to evenly distribute the paint and remove any excess.
- Apply the paint using long, sweeping strokes, working from one side to the other and from top to bottom. Use gentle but consistent pressure to ensure even coverage and avoid drips or runs.
- Roll back over the painted surface in the opposite direction to smooth out any ridges or texture left by the roller.

3. Applicators:

Paint applicators such as paint pads, edgers, and sprayers are specialized tools designed for specific painting tasks and surfaces. Here's an overview of common paint applicators and their uses:

- Paint Pads: Paint pads feature a flat, rectangular surface with a built-in reservoir for holding paint. They are ideal for painting large, flat surfaces such as walls and ceilings and provide smooth, even coverage with minimal splatter.
- Edgers: Edgers are designed for cutting-in and detail work around edges, corners, and trim. They feature a shielded edge or guide wheel that prevents paint from bleeding onto adjacent surfaces, ensuring clean and precise lines.

- Sprayers: Paint sprayers use compressed air or high pressure to atomize paint and apply it evenly to surfaces. They are ideal for painting large areas quickly and efficiently and provide smooth, professional-quality results with minimal effort.

By understanding the features, uses, and techniques of brushes, rollers, and applicators, you can confidently select the right tools for your painting projects and achieve professional-quality results with ease. Whether you're painting walls, trim, or furniture, having the right tools and mastering their use is essential for achieving optimal efficiency and a flawless finish. So stock up on brushes, rollers, and applicators, and let your creativity shine as you transform your space with paint!

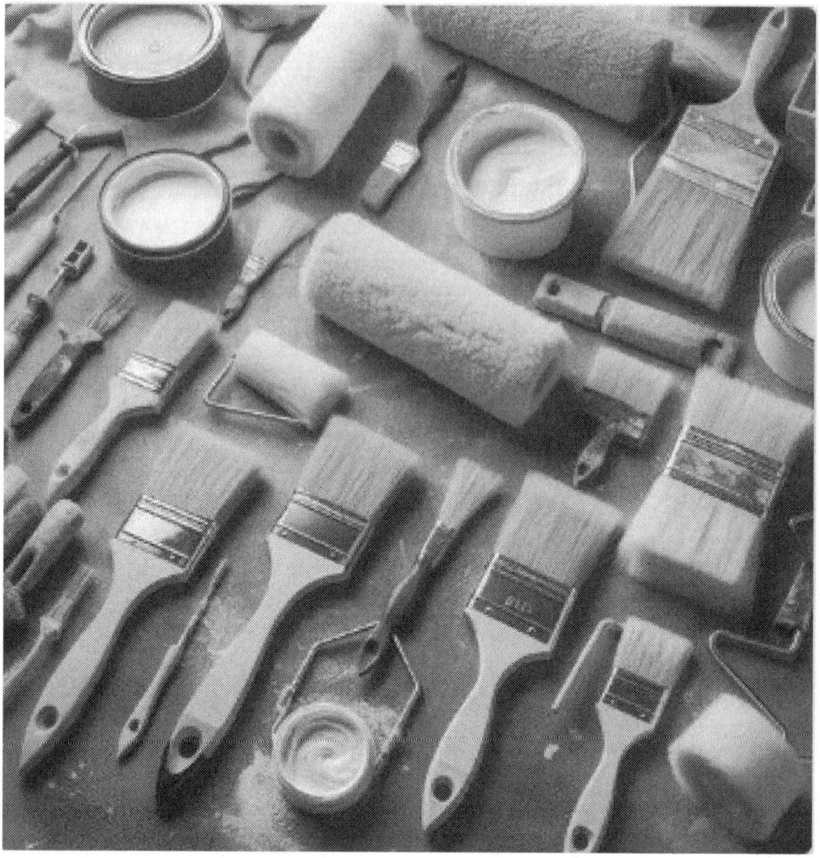

Masking and Protective Equipment

Masking and protective equipment are essential for ensuring safety, cleanliness, and precision during painting projects. Whether you're painting walls, trim, or furniture, proper masking and protective equipment help protect surfaces, minimize mess, and safeguard your health. In this section, we'll provide a detailed explanation of masking and protective equipment, guiding you through their features, uses, and techniques to ensure success in your painting endeavors.

1. Painter's Tape:
Painter's tape is a versatile masking tool designed to protect surfaces from paint splatter and ensure clean, crisp lines. Here's an overview of painter's tape and its uses:

Features:
- Low-tack Adhesive: Painter's tape features a low-tack adhesive that adheres securely to surfaces without causing damage or leaving behind residue.
- Easy Removal: Painter's tape is designed to be easily removed without tearing or lifting paint, making it ideal for temporary masking and protection.
- Various Widths: Painter's tape comes in various widths to accommodate different surfaces and masking needs, from narrow trim to wide walls and ceilings.

Uses:

Masking Trim: Use painter's tape to mask off trim, baseboards, and molding before painting walls or ceilings. Apply the tape along the edge of the trim, pressing it down firmly to ensure a tight seal and prevent paint bleed.

- Creating Straight Lines: Use painter's tape to create straight lines and sharp edges when painting stripes, patterns, or accent walls. Apply the tape in a straight line, using a level or straight edge as a guide for precision.
- Protecting Surfaces: Use painter's tape to protect surfaces such as windows, doors, and fixtures from paint splatter and overspray. Apply the tape around the perimeter of the surface, overlapping each piece slightly to ensure full coverage.

2. Plastic Sheeting:

Plastic sheeting is a durable and flexible protective barrier that helps contain paint splatter and overspray, making cleanup easier and minimizing mess. Here's an overview of plastic sheeting and its uses:

Features:

- Lightweight and Flexible: Plastic sheeting is lightweight and flexible, making it easy to drape over furniture, floors, and fixtures for protection.
- Tear-resistant: Plastic sheeting is tear-resistant and puncture-proof, providing reliable protection against paint splatter and spills.
- Disposable: Plastic sheeting is disposable, making cleanup quick and convenient. Simply roll up the sheeting and dispose of it after use.

Uses:
- Protecting Floors: Use plastic sheeting to cover floors and carpets during painting projects to prevent paint splatter and spills. Lay the sheeting flat and secure it in place with painter's tape or masking tape around the perimeter.
- Covering Furniture: Use plastic sheeting to cover furniture and fixtures to protect them from paint splatter and overspray. Drape the sheeting over the furniture and secure it in place with tape or plastic clips.
- Creating Spray Booths: Use plastic sheeting to create temporary spray booths for spray painting projects. Enclose the area with plastic sheeting to contain overspray and minimize contamination of surrounding surfaces.

3. Personal Protective Equipment (PPE):

Personal protective equipment (PPE) helps protect painters from exposure to hazardous chemicals, fumes, and airborne particles during painting projects. Here's an overview of PPE and its uses:

Features:
- Respiratory Protection: Respirators and masks help protect painters from inhaling paint fumes, dust, and other airborne particles. Choose a respirator or mask with appropriate filtration levels for the type of paint and environment.
- Eye Protection: Safety goggles or glasses protect painters from eye irritation and injury caused by paint splatter, dust, and debris. Choose goggles with impact-resistant lenses and a snug, comfortable fit.

- Skin Protection: Gloves and coveralls help protect painters' skin from exposure to paint, solvents, and other chemicals. Choose gloves made from nitrile or latex for chemical resistance and coveralls made from durable, breathable materials for comfort and protection.

Uses:
- Respiratory Protection: Wear a respirator or mask when painting in poorly ventilated areas or when using paints, primers, or finishes that emit strong fumes. Ensure that the respirator or mask forms a tight seal against the face to provide maximum protection.
- Eye Protection: Wear safety goggles or glasses whenever painting overhead or in areas with potential for paint splatter and debris. Choose goggles with anti-fog lenses and adjustable straps for a secure fit.
- Skin Protection: Wear gloves and coveralls to protect your skin from contact with paint, solvents, and other chemicals. Choose gloves that fit snugly and coveralls that provide full-body coverage and freedom of movement.

By understanding the features, uses, and techniques of masking and protective equipment, you can ensure safety, cleanliness, and precision during your painting projects. Whether you're painting walls, trim, or furniture, proper masking and protective equipment help protect surfaces, minimize mess, and safeguard your health. So stock up on painter's tape, plastic sheeting, and personal protective equipment, and paint with confidence—your freshly painted space awaits!

Specialty Tools for Specific Surfaces

Specialty tools for specific surfaces are essential for achieving professional-quality results and overcoming unique challenges encountered during painting projects. Whether you're painting textured surfaces, intricate trim, or hard-to-reach areas, having the right tools for the job can make all the difference in achieving optimal efficiency and a flawless finish. In this section, we'll provide a detailed explanation of specialty tools for specific surfaces, guiding you through their features, uses, and techniques to ensure success in your painting endeavors.

1. Textured Surface Tools:
Textured surfaces such as stucco, brick, and textured wallpaper require specialized tools for effective paint application and coverage. Here's an overview of specialty tools for painting textured surfaces:

- Texture Rollers: Texture rollers feature raised patterns or textures that imprint onto the painted surface, creating decorative effects and adding visual interest. Choose texture rollers with varying patterns and depths to achieve different textures and finishes.
- Stippling Brushes: Stippling brushes are designed to create textured effects by dabbing or stippling paint onto the surface. They feature coarse bristles or foam pads that create a stippled or stipple-like texture when applied to the surface.
- Texture Sprayers: Texture sprayers use compressed air or high pressure to atomize paint and apply it evenly to textured surfaces.

- They feature adjustable nozzles and spray patterns to accommodate different textures and viscosities, ensuring consistent coverage and a uniform finish.

Techniques:
- Use texture rollers to apply paint to textured surfaces, rolling the roller over the surface in a consistent pattern to create uniform texture and coverage.
- Use stippling brushes to dab or stipple paint onto the surface, working in small sections and overlapping each application to blend the texture seamlessly.
- Use texture sprayers to apply paint evenly to textured surfaces, adjusting the spray pattern and flow rate to achieve the desired texture and coverage.

2. Trim and Detail Tools:
Trim and detail work require precision and accuracy to achieve clean lines and sharp edges. Here's an overview of specialty tools for painting trim and detail work:

- Edging Tools: Edging tools such as paint edgers and trim guides help create clean, straight lines and sharp edges when cutting in around trim, molding, and other detailed areas. They feature built-in guides or shields that prevent paint from bleeding onto adjacent surfaces, ensuring precise results.
- Artist Brushes: Artist brushes are small, fine-tipped brushes designed for detail work and intricate painting tasks. They feature thin, flexible bristles that allow for precise control and application of paint, making them ideal for painting trim, accents, and fine details.

- Detail Rollers: Detail rollers are small, narrow rollers designed for painting trim, molding, and other detailed areas. They feature a compact design and fine nap length, allowing for precise application and smooth coverage in tight spaces.

Techniques:
- Use edging tools to cut in around trim, molding, and other detailed areas, pressing the guide firmly against the surface to create a seal and prevent paint bleed.
- Use artist brushes to paint fine details, accents, and intricate designs, using short, controlled strokes for precise application.
- Use detail rollers to paint trim and molding, rolling the roller evenly along the surface to achieve smooth, uniform coverage in tight spaces.

3. High Reach and Hard-to-Reach Tools:

High reach and hard-to-reach areas such as ceilings, walls, and stairwells require specialized tools for safe and efficient paint application. Here's an overview of specialty tools for painting high reach and hard-to-reach areas:

- Extension Poles: Extension poles attach to paint rollers, brushes, or applicators to extend your reach and access high or hard-to-reach areas such as ceilings and tall walls. They feature telescoping or adjustable lengths for versatility and ease of use.

- Ladder Accessories: Ladder accessories such as ladder stabilizers, standoff brackets, and ladder jacks provide stability and safety when working on ladders. They attach to the ladder to create a secure platform for painting high or hard-to-reach areas.
- Pivot Tools: Pivot tools such as pivot rollers and pivot brushes feature swivel heads or adjustable angles that allow for easy maneuverability and access to angled or uneven surfaces. They are ideal for painting stairwells, sloped ceilings, and other challenging areas.

Techniques:
- Use extension poles to access high or hard-to-reach areas such as ceilings and tall walls, extending your reach and reducing the need for ladders or scaffolding.
- Use ladder accessories to stabilize and secure your ladder when working on high or hard-to-reach areas, ensuring safety and stability during painting projects.
- Use pivot tools to access angled or uneven surfaces, adjusting the angle or swivel head to accommodate challenging areas and achieve even coverage.

By understanding the features, uses, and techniques of specialty tools for specific surfaces, you can confidently tackle any painting project and achieve professional-quality results with ease. Whether you're painting textured surfaces, intricate trim, or hard-to-reach areas, having the right tools for the job ensures optimal efficiency, precision, and safety. So stock up on texture rollers, edging tools, extension poles, and other specialty tools, and paint with confidence—your freshly painted space awaits!

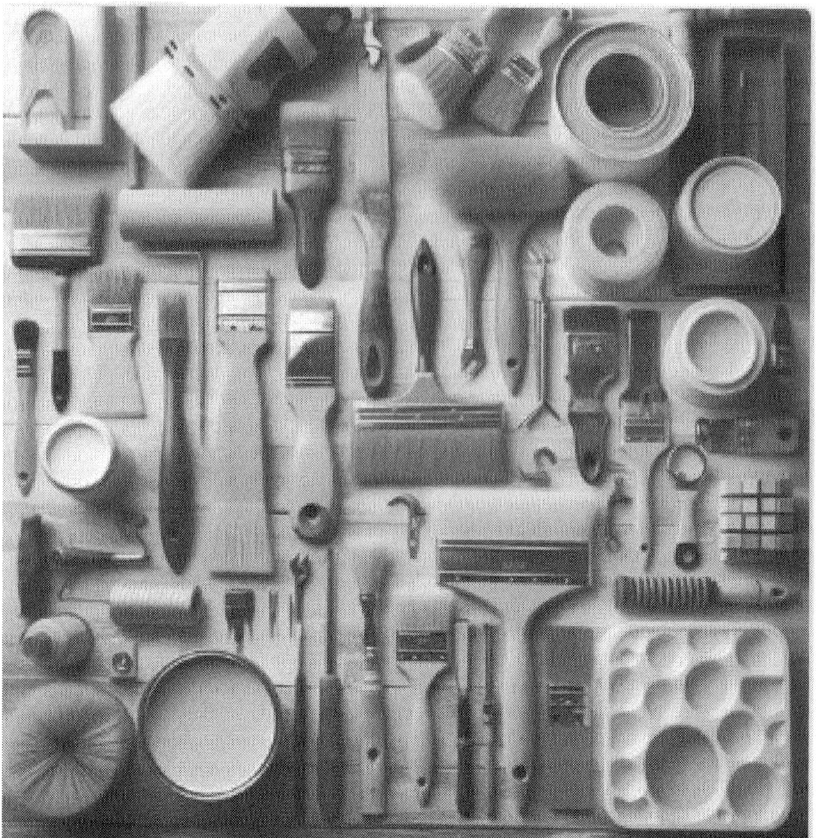

Chapter 5
Troubleshooting Common Issues
Dealing with Drips and Runs

Dealing with drips and runs is a common challenge encountered during painting projects, but with the right techniques and solutions, you can easily address and prevent these issues to achieve a flawless finish. In this section, we'll provide a detailed explanation of how to troubleshoot and deal with drips and runs effectively.

1. Identify the Cause:
Before addressing drips and runs, it's essential to understand the underlying causes to prevent them from recurring. Common causes of drips and runs include:
- Overloading the brush or roller with paint.
- Applying too much pressure or using too thick of a coat of paint.
- Painting in hot or humid conditions, which can cause the paint to dry too quickly.
- Using old or expired paint that has thickened or separated.
- Painting on a surface that is not properly prepared or primed.

2. Immediate Action:
If you notice drips or runs while painting, take immediate action to address them before the paint dries and becomes difficult to fix. Here's what you can do:
- Stop painting immediately and assess the extent of the drips or runs.

- Use a clean brush or roller to smooth out the excess paint and redistribute it evenly across the surface.
- If the drips or runs are small, you can often blend them into the surrounding area by feathering out the edges with a dry brush or roller.
- If the drips or runs are significant, carefully remove excess paint with a putty knife or scraper, taking care not to damage the underlying surface.

3. Prevention Techniques:
Preventing drips and runs before they occur is the best approach to achieving a smooth, even finish. Here are some techniques to help prevent drips and runs during painting:
- Load the brush or roller with a moderate amount of paint, tapping off any excess on the side of the paint tray or can.
- Use light, even pressure when applying paint to the surface, avoiding pressing too hard or applying too thick of a coat.
- Work in small sections and maintain a wet edge to prevent paint from drying too quickly and causing drips or runs.
- Use a high-quality paint with good flow and leveling properties to minimize the risk of drips and runs.
- Paint in moderate temperature and humidity conditions, ideally between 50°F to 85°F with low humidity, to ensure optimal drying and adhesion of the paint.

4. *Touch-up and Repair:*
If drips or runs occur despite your best efforts to prevent them, don't worry—most issues can be easily fixed with some touch-up and repair work. Here's how to address drips and runs after the paint has dried:
- Sand down the affected area with fine-grit sandpaper to smooth out the surface and remove any excess paint.
- Wipe away sanding dust with a clean, damp cloth and allow the surface to dry completely.
- Apply a thin coat of paint to the affected area using a brush or roller, feathering out the edges to blend it seamlessly with the surrounding area.
- Allow the touch-up paint to dry completely before inspecting the surface for any additional touch-ups or repairs needed.

By understanding the causes of drips and runs and implementing prevention techniques, you can minimize the risk of these common painting issues and achieve professional-quality results with ease. In the event that drips or runs occur, taking immediate action and employing touch-up and repair techniques will help you restore the surface to its desired finish. So keep these troubleshooting tips in mind as you tackle your next painting project, and paint with confidence—drips and runs don't stand a chance against your expertise!

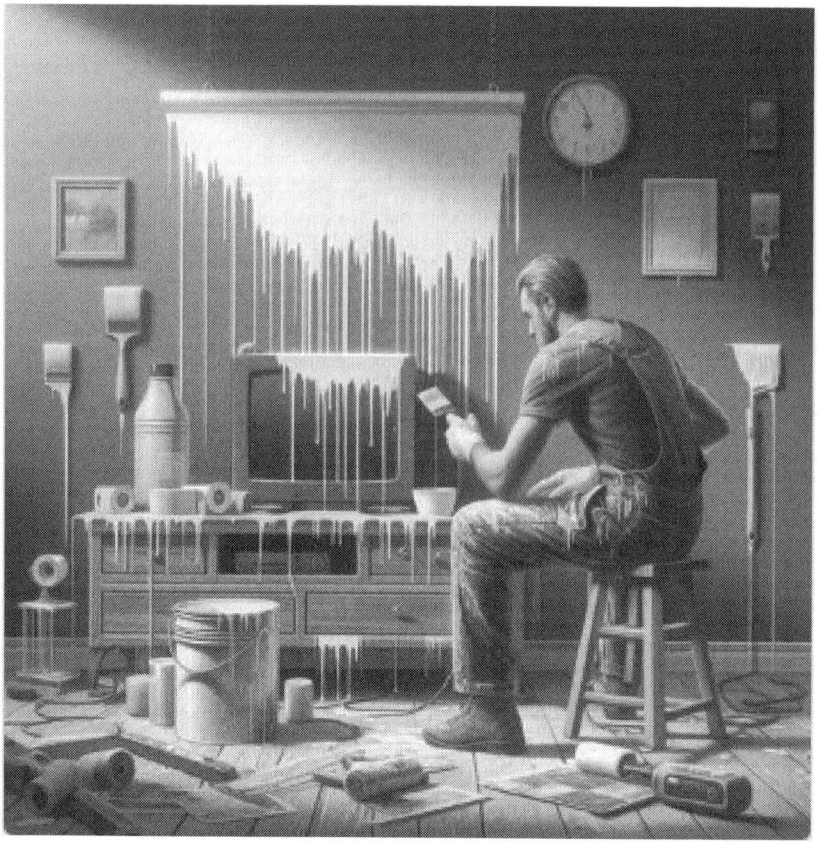

Achieving Smooth Finishes

Achieving smooth finishes is a key goal in any painting project, whether you're painting walls, trim, furniture, or other surfaces. A smooth finish enhances the appearance of the painted surface, providing a professional-looking result. In this section, we'll explore techniques and tips to help you achieve smooth finishes in your painting projects.

1. Surface Preparation:
Smooth finishes start with proper surface preparation. Here's how to prepare surfaces for painting:
- Clean the surface thoroughly to remove dirt, dust, grease, and other contaminants that can affect paint adhesion and finish.
- Repair any imperfections such as cracks, holes, or dents with spackling compound or wood filler. Sand the repaired areas smooth once dry.
- Sand the entire surface with fine-grit sandpaper to smooth out rough spots, uneven textures, and previous paint drips or runs.
- Remove any sanding dust with a tack cloth or damp cloth before painting to ensure a clean surface.

2. Primer Application:
Using a high-quality primer is essential for achieving smooth finishes, especially on porous or uneven surfaces. Here's how to apply primer effectively:
- Choose a primer that is suitable for the surface you're painting and compatible with the type of paint you'll be using.

- Apply the primer evenly using a brush, roller, or sprayer, working in small sections from top to bottom and from one side to the other.
- Use long, smooth strokes to apply the primer, overlapping each stroke slightly to ensure even coverage.
- Allow the primer to dry completely according to the manufacturer's instructions before applying paint.

3. Paint Application:
Proper paint application is crucial for achieving smooth finishes. Here's how to apply paint effectively:
- Use high-quality paint that is appropriate for the surface you're painting and the desired finish.
- Stir the paint thoroughly before application to ensure an even consistency and proper color dispersion.
- Load the brush or roller with a moderate amount of paint, tapping off any excess on the side of the paint tray or can.
- Apply the paint evenly using long, smooth strokes, working in small sections and maintaining a wet edge to prevent lap marks and streaks.
- Use light, even pressure when applying paint to avoid drips, runs, and uneven coverage.
- If using a roller, roll the roller in a W-shaped pattern or zigzag motion to evenly distribute the paint and avoid creating visible lines or streaks.
- Feather out the edges of each stroke to blend them together and eliminate any visible brush marks or roller lines.

4. Sanding and Finishing:
After the paint has dried completely, sanding and finishing are essential for achieving a smooth, flawless finish. Here's how to finish the painted surface effectively:
- Inspect the painted surface for any imperfections such as brush marks, roller lines, or drips.
- Lightly sand the surface with fine-grit sandpaper to smooth out any rough spots or imperfections. Be careful not to sand through the paint layer.
- Wipe away sanding dust with a tack cloth or damp cloth and allow the surface to dry completely.
- Apply additional coats of paint as needed to achieve the desired finish, following the same techniques for paint application.
- For an extra-smooth finish, consider applying a clear topcoat or varnish to protect the painted surface and enhance its appearance.

By following these techniques and tips for surface preparation, primer application, paint application, and finishing, you can achieve smooth finishes in your painting projects with confidence. Remember to take your time, work carefully, and pay attention to detail for professional-quality results that enhance the beauty of your space. So grab your paintbrushes and rollers, and paint with confidence—smooth finishes await!

ADDRESSING UNEVEN COVERAGE

Addressing uneven coverage is essential for achieving a professional-quality finish in your painting projects. Uneven coverage can result in blotchy or patchy areas that detract from the overall appearance of the painted surface. In this section, we'll explore techniques and tips to help you address and correct uneven coverage effectively.

1. Identify the Cause:
Before addressing uneven coverage, it's important to identify the underlying causes to prevent recurrence. Common causes of uneven coverage include:

- Inadequate surface preparation: Uneven surfaces, dirt, dust, or grease can affect paint adhesion and result in uneven coverage.
- Incorrect application technique: Applying paint too thinly or too thickly, using the wrong type of brush or roller, or using improper pressure can lead to uneven coverage.
- Low-quality paint: Using low-quality or expired paint with poor coverage properties can result in uneven coverage and poor adhesion.

2. Immediate Action:
If you notice uneven coverage while painting, take immediate action to address it before the paint dries and becomes difficult to fix. Here's what you can do:

- Stop painting immediately and assess the extent of the uneven coverage.

- Reload the brush or roller with paint and apply an additional coat to the uneven areas, focusing on blending the paint into the surrounding areas for seamless coverage.
- Use long, smooth strokes and apply light, even pressure to ensure uniform coverage and avoid creating additional streaks or patches.
- If the uneven coverage persists, allow the paint to dry completely before applying additional coats to build up coverage gradually.

3. Prevention Techniques:
Preventing uneven coverage before it occurs is the best approach to achieving a smooth, uniform finish. Here are some techniques to help prevent uneven coverage during painting:
- Proper surface preparation: Ensure the surface is clean, smooth, and free of dirt, dust, grease, and other contaminants before painting. Repair any imperfections and sand the surface smooth to promote even paint adhesion.
- Use high-quality paint: Invest in high-quality paint with good coverage properties and color consistency to ensure uniform coverage and durability.
- Choose the right tools: Select brushes, rollers, and applicators suitable for the type of paint and surface you're painting. Use brushes with fine bristles for smooth surfaces and rollers with the appropriate nap length for textured surfaces.

- Apply paint evenly: Use long, smooth strokes and apply paint evenly across the surface, working in small sections and maintaining a wet edge to prevent lap marks and streaks.

4. Touch-up and Repair:
If uneven coverage occurs despite your best efforts to prevent it, don't worry—most issues can be easily fixed with some touch-up and repair work. Here's how to address uneven coverage after the paint has dried:
- Sand down the affected areas with fine-grit sandpaper to smooth out any rough spots or imperfections and promote adhesion of additional coats.
- Wipe away sanding dust with a tack cloth or damp cloth and allow the surface to dry completely.
- Apply additional coats of paint to the uneven areas, using the same techniques for paint application as before. Blend the paint into the surrounding areas for seamless coverage and uniform finish.
- Allow the paint to dry completely between coats and inspect the surface for any remaining unevenness or imperfections. Repeat the touch-up process as needed until you achieve the desired coverage and finish.

By understanding the causes of uneven coverage and implementing prevention techniques, you can minimize the risk of this common painting issue and achieve professional-quality results with ease. In the event that uneven coverage occurs, taking immediate action and employing touch-up and repair techniques will help you correct the issue and achieve a smooth, uniform finish.

So keep these troubleshooting tips in mind as you tackle your next painting project, and paint with confidence—uneven coverage doesn't stand a chance against your expertise!

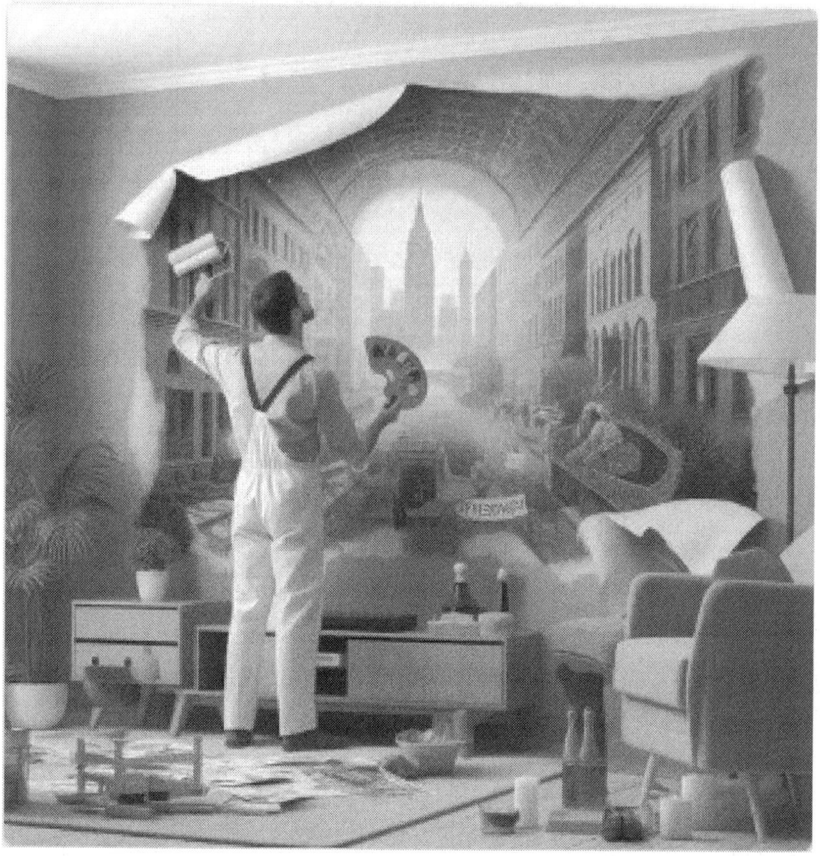

Chapter 6
Advanced Techniques and Finishing Touches
Faux Finishes and Decorative Painting

Advanced techniques such as faux finishes and decorative painting add depth, texture, and visual interest to your painted surfaces, elevating them from ordinary to extraordinary. These techniques allow you to mimic the appearance of natural materials, create intricate patterns, or add artistic flair to your space. In this section, we'll explore faux finishes and decorative painting in detail, providing step-by-step instructions and tips for achieving stunning results.

1. Faux Finishes:
Faux finishes are decorative painting techniques that replicate the look and texture of natural materials such as wood, stone, marble, or leather. With faux finishes, you can transform ordinary surfaces into luxurious and sophisticated focal points. Here are some popular faux finish techniques:

- Faux Wood Grain: Create the rich, warm look of wood grain on surfaces such as doors, trim, or furniture using a faux wood grain technique. This technique involves layering paint colors and using specialized tools such as a wood graining tool or a dry brush to create realistic wood grain patterns.

- Faux Marble: Achieve the elegant, timeless beauty of marble on surfaces such as countertops, tabletops, or fireplace surrounds using a faux marble technique. This technique involves layering paint colors and using feathering or veining techniques to mimic the natural veining and movement of marble.
- Faux Stone: Capture the rugged, earthy texture of stone on surfaces such as walls, pillars, or accent features using a faux stone technique. This technique involves layering paint colors and using sponging or stippling techniques to create the look of natural stone textures and variations.
- Faux Leather: Add warmth and sophistication to surfaces such as walls or furniture using a faux leather technique. This technique involves layering paint colors and using specialized tools such as a leather graining tool or a stippling brush to create the look of supple leather textures.

2. Decorative Painting:
Decorative painting encompasses a wide range of artistic techniques and styles that allow you to personalize and enhance your space with custom designs, patterns, or motifs. From intricate stenciling to freehand murals, decorative painting offers endless possibilities for creativity and expression. Here are some popular decorative painting techniques:

- Stenciling: Stenciling involves using pre-cut or custom-made stencils to apply paint designs, patterns, or motifs to surfaces such as walls, furniture, or floors.

- Stenciling is a versatile and easy-to-master technique that allows you to create repeatable patterns and intricate designs with precision.
- Trompe l'Oeil: Trompe l'Oeil, which means "deceive the eye" in French, is a decorative painting technique that creates optical illusions to make two-dimensional surfaces appear three-dimensional. Trompe l'Oeil techniques can be used to create realistic architectural elements, landscapes, or still-life scenes that add depth and dimension to your space.
- Mural Painting: Mural painting involves creating large-scale paintings or murals directly on walls or ceilings to transform the entire space into a work of art. Mural painting allows you to express your creativity on a grand scale and can be customized to suit any theme, style, or aesthetic.
- Faux Finishes and Glazes: Incorporate faux finishes and glazes into your decorative painting projects to add depth, texture, and visual interest to surfaces. Faux finishes and glazes can be used to create subtle color variations, aged patinas, or distressed effects that enhance the overall look and feel of your space.

3. Tips for Success:
- Practice on sample boards or scrap materials before attempting faux finishes or decorative painting techniques on your actual project to perfect your skills and experiment with different colors and textures.
- Invest in high-quality paint, brushes, and tools specifically designed for faux finishes and decorative painting to ensure optimal results and durability.

- Take your time and work methodically, following the instructions and techniques for each faux finish or decorative painting technique to achieve the desired effect.
- Experiment with different color combinations, layering techniques, and finishing touches to personalize your faux finishes and decorative painting projects and make them uniquely your own.

By mastering faux finishes and decorative painting techniques, you can transform ordinary surfaces into extraordinary works of art that reflect your personal style and creativity. Whether you're adding warmth and texture with faux wood grain or making a bold statement with a custom mural, the possibilities for expression and innovation are endless. So unleash your creativity, explore new techniques, and elevate your space with the beauty and sophistication of faux finishes and decorative painting!

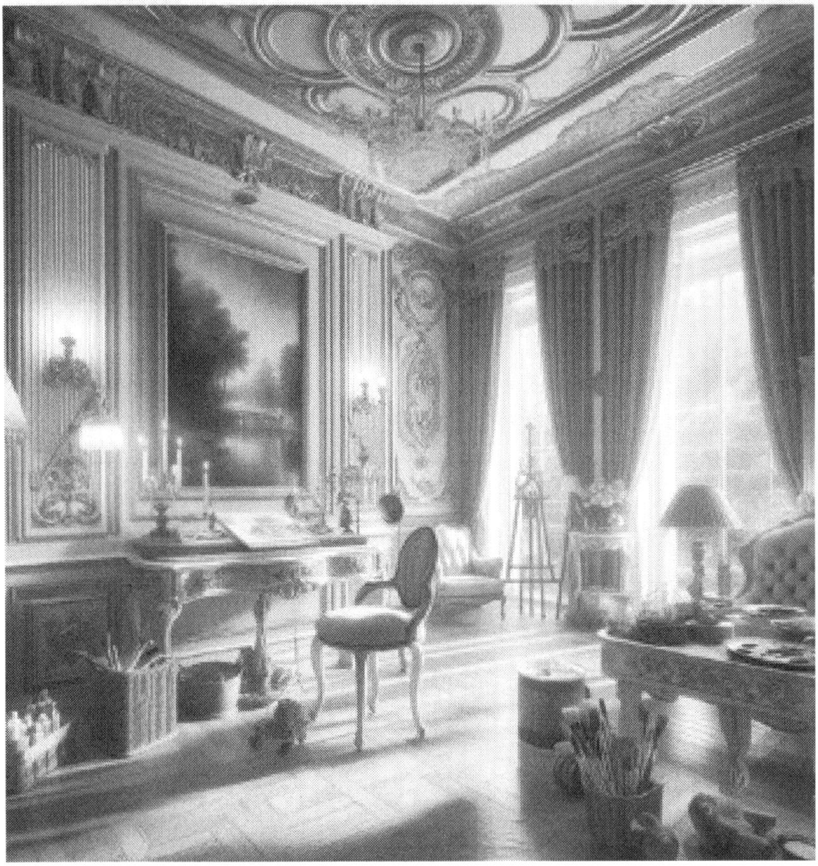

Adding Texture to Walls

Adding texture to walls is a versatile way to enhance the visual appeal and character of any room in your home or office. Textured walls not only add depth and interest to the space but also provide a unique backdrop for furniture, artwork, and decor. From subtle textures to bold patterns, there are various techniques you can use to achieve textured walls. In this comprehensive guide, we'll explore different methods for adding texture to walls, along with tips and tricks for each technique.

1. Textured Paint:
Textured paint is a popular option for adding texture to walls, offering a simple and cost-effective way to achieve various textured effects. Textured paint contains additives such as sand, silica, or cellulose fibers that create texture when applied to the wall surface. Here's how to use textured paint effectively:

- Choose the right textured paint: Textured paints come in different finishes, from fine to coarse textures. Consider the desired texture and aesthetic of your space when selecting the paint.
- Prepare the wall surface: Clean the walls thoroughly to remove any dirt, dust, or grease. Repair any cracks or holes and sand the surface smooth if necessary. Prime the walls with a suitable primer to ensure proper adhesion of the textured paint.
- Apply the textured paint: Use a roller, brush, or sprayer to apply the textured paint to the walls. Work in small sections, starting from the top and working your way down. Use overlapping strokes to ensure even coverage and texture.

- Experiment with application techniques: Depending on the desired texture, you can apply the textured paint using various techniques such as stippling, swirling, or dabbing. Test different techniques on a small section of the wall to find the desired effect.

2. Venetian Plaster:

Venetian plaster is a luxurious and sophisticated wall finish that adds depth and elegance to any space. Made from natural materials such as marble dust and lime putty, Venetian plaster creates a smooth, polished surface with subtle variations in color and texture. Here's how to apply Venetian plaster:

- Prepare the wall surface: Clean the walls and repair any imperfections. Apply a base coat of primer or tinted plaster to create a smooth and even base for the Venetian plaster.
- Apply the Venetian plaster: Use a trowel to apply the Venetian plaster in thin, overlapping layers. Work in small sections and use a variety of application techniques such as troweling, swirling, or stippling to create texture and depth.
- Burnish the plaster: Once the Venetian plaster is dry, use a trowel or polishing tool to burnish the surface. This will smooth out any imperfections and create a glossy, reflective finish.
- Seal the plaster: Apply a protective sealer or wax to the Venetian plaster to enhance durability and protect the surface from damage.

3. Faux Finishes:

Faux finishes are decorative painting techniques that replicate the look of natural materials such as stone, brick, or wood on walls. Faux finishes offer endless possibilities for adding texture and visual interest to walls. Here's how to create faux finishes on walls:

- Choose the right technique: Select a faux finish technique that complements the style and aesthetic of your space. Popular faux finish techniques include sponging, ragging, stippling, dragging, and combing.
- Prepare the wall surface: Clean and prime the walls to ensure proper adhesion of the faux finish. Apply a base coat of solid color paint that complements the faux finish.
- Apply the faux finish: Use a variety of tools such as sponges, rags, brushes, or specialty tools to apply the faux finish paint. Experiment with different application techniques to achieve the desired texture and effect.
- Seal the finish: Once the faux finish is dry, apply a protective topcoat or sealer to enhance durability and protect the surface from damage.

By exploring these techniques for adding texture to walls, you can transform ordinary walls into extraordinary focal points that enhance the beauty and character of your space. Whether you prefer subtle textures or bold patterns, there's a textured wall option to suit every style and aesthetic. So unleash your creativity, experiment with different techniques, and elevate your walls to new heights of style and sophistication!

Finalizing Details for Professional Results

Finalizing details is a crucial step in achieving professional results in any painting project. Paying attention to the finer details ensures that your work appears polished, cohesive, and visually appealing. In this section, we'll explore various aspects of finalizing details to help you achieve a professional finish.

1. Touch-Up Work:
After completing the main painting tasks, it's essential to inspect the entire surface for any imperfections or inconsistencies that may have been missed. Here's how to approach touch-up work effectively:

- Identify areas that require touch-up: Look for uneven coverage, drips, runs, or other blemishes that detract from the overall appearance of the painted surface.
- Address imperfections: Use fine-grit sandpaper to smooth out rough spots or imperfections. Clean the surface thoroughly to remove any sanding dust, then touch up the affected areas with additional paint as needed.
- Blend touch-up areas: Feather out the edges of the touch-up paint to blend it seamlessly with the surrounding area, ensuring a smooth and uniform finish.

2. Clean-Up:
Proper clean-up is essential for maintaining a tidy work environment and preserving the quality of your painting tools. Here's how to clean up effectively:

- Clean brushes and rollers: Thoroughly rinse brushes and rollers with warm, soapy water to remove paint residue. Use a brush comb or wire brush to remove paint from bristles or nap, then rinse again until the water runs clear. Allow brushes and rollers to dry completely before storing.
- Dispose of paint properly: Dispose of leftover paint according to local regulations. Seal paint cans tightly to prevent spills or leaks, and store them in a cool, dry place away from direct sunlight.
- Clean work area: Wipe down surfaces with a damp cloth to remove any paint splatters or spills. Vacuum or sweep the floor to remove dust and debris.

3. Inspect and Evaluate:
Take the time to step back and evaluate your work once the paint has dried completely. Here's what to consider during the inspection process:
- Check for uniformity: Ensure that the paint coverage is consistent and uniform across the entire surface. Look for any areas that may appear lighter or darker than others and touch up as needed.
- Evaluate transitions: Pay attention to transitions between different colors or textures, such as where two walls meet or where trim meets the wall. Make any necessary adjustments to ensure smooth transitions and seamless integration.
- Assess overall appearance: Step back and view the painted surface from different angles and lighting conditions. Consider how the finished result complements the rest of the space and whether any additional adjustments are needed.

- Clean brushes and rollers: Thoroughly rinse brushes and rollers with warm, soapy water to remove paint residue. Use a brush comb or wire brush to remove paint from bristles or nap, then rinse again until the water runs clear. Allow brushes and rollers to dry completely before storing.
- Dispose of paint properly: Dispose of leftover paint according to local regulations. Seal paint cans tightly to prevent spills or leaks, and store them in a cool, dry place away from direct sunlight.
- Clean work area: Wipe down surfaces with a damp cloth to remove any paint splatters or spills. Vacuum or sweep the floor to remove dust and debris.

3. Inspect and Evaluate:
Take the time to step back and evaluate your work once the paint has dried completely. Here's what to consider during the inspection process:
- Check for uniformity: Ensure that the paint coverage is consistent and uniform across the entire surface. Look for any areas that may appear lighter or darker than others and touch up as needed.
- Evaluate transitions: Pay attention to transitions between different colors or textures, such as where two walls meet or where trim meets the wall. Make any necessary adjustments to ensure smooth transitions and seamless integration.
- Assess overall appearance: Step back and view the painted surface from different angles and lighting conditions. Consider how the finished result complements the rest of the space and whether any additional adjustments are needed.

4. Final Details:

Once you're satisfied with the overall appearance of the painted surface, it's time to attend to final details that can elevate the finish to a professional level. Here are some final details to consider:

- Paint trim and accents: Apply paint to trim, moldings, baseboards, and other architectural details to complete the look of the room. Use a steady hand and fine-tipped brush for precision.
- Add decorative touches: Consider adding decorative elements such as stencils, borders, or murals to enhance the visual interest of the painted surface. Use painter's tape to create crisp lines and clean edges.
- Protect and maintain: Apply a clear topcoat or sealer to protect the painted surface from wear and tear. Consider using washable or scrubbable paint finishes in high-traffic areas for added durability.

By focusing on finalizing details, you can ensure that your painting project achieves professional-quality results that stand the test of time. Taking the time to address touch-ups, clean up properly, inspect and evaluate the finished surface, and attend to final details will help you achieve a flawless finish that enhances the beauty and value of your space. So approach the finalization process with care and attention to detail, and enjoy the satisfaction of a job well done!

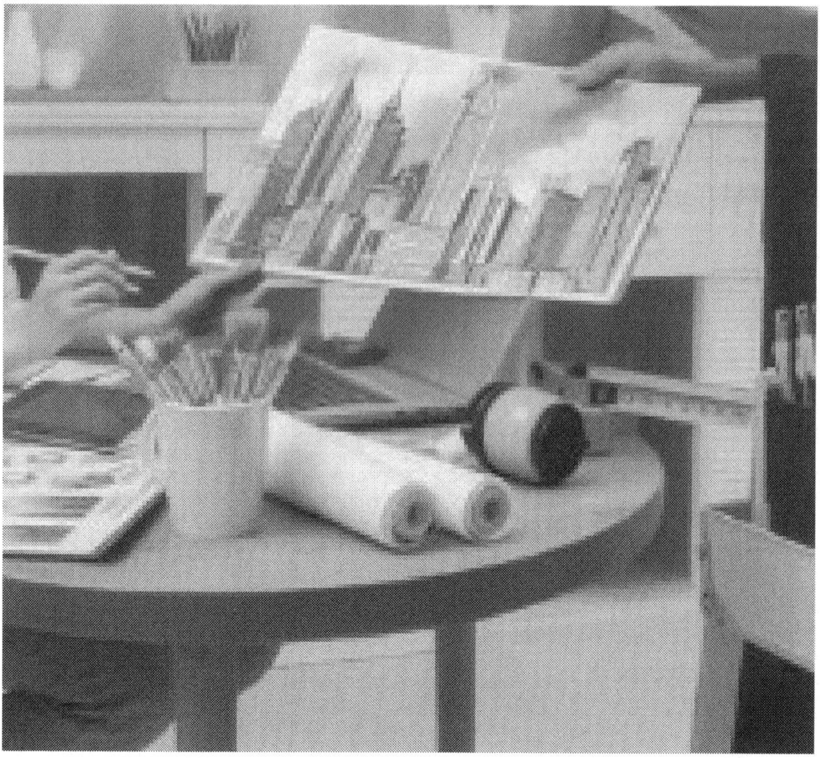

CONCLUSION

In conclusion, "How to Paint Interiors - Prepare, Choose Colors, Apply Techniques, and Use Tools" has equipped you with the knowledge and skills needed to embark on successful interior painting projects with confidence and expertise. Throughout this comprehensive guide, we've delved into the intricacies of surface preparation, color selection, paint application methods, and essential painting tools, providing you with detailed explanations, practical tips, and step-by-step instructions every step of the way.

From mastering surface preparation techniques to achieving smooth finishes, addressing common issues, and adding texture to walls, each chapter has been meticulously crafted to empower you to tackle any painting project with ease and precision. Whether you're a novice painter looking to enhance your home or a seasoned DIY enthusiast seeking to refine your skills, this book serves as your indispensable companion on your journey to achieving flawless results.

As you apply the knowledge and techniques gleaned from these pages, remember that painting is both an art and a science—a creative endeavor that requires patience, attention to detail, and a touch of inspiration. Embrace the opportunity to transform your surroundings, express your personal style, and breathe new life into your living spaces through the transformative power of paint.

With dedication, practice, and a willingness to explore new possibilities, you'll discover the joy and satisfaction that come from creating beautiful, professionally finished interiors that reflect your unique personality and vision. So pick up your brushes, select your colors, and embark on your painting journey with confidence, knowing that the skills and insights gained from this book will serve as your trusted companions every step of the way.

May your painting endeavors be filled with creativity, success, and the fulfillment of bringing your vision to life. Here's to many happy hours of painting and to the transformative beauty that awaits within the walls of your home.

Made in the USA
Columbia, SC
27 December 2024